MEGA BOOK O

MW00880688

MAHINROOP PM

Introduction

"Mega Book of Website Designing" helps to get a deeper understanding of website designing. It is an absolute must read for web designers, internet marketers, web developers and Information Technology professionals. Anyone who is planning to build or already has a website will immensely benefit from this book. List of topics covered in the book include flash website designing, mobile website designing, website designing ideas for small business, responsive website designing, open source website designing, ecommerce website designing and Photoshop basics.

About the Author

MAHINROOP PM is an Information Technology consultant based in India. He holds bachelors degree in Computer Science Engineering and masters degree in Business Administration. The author is passionate about technology, ecommerce, websites and books.

Written by MAHINROOP PM

Table of Contents

Introduction to Website Designing

An ideal website should be appealing to both the visitors and search engines alike so that they rank high in the search engine results. There are three types of website designing: static, dynamic and electronic commerce websites. Static design is best if we need few pages on our website and don't want the information to change. Static websites can be created in HTML (Hypertext Mark Up Language) and CSS (Cascading Style Sheets). It is very easy to develop static websites and they can be easily indexed by search engines.

A dynamic website is built on content management systems including WordPress, Joomla and Drupal. Drupal is an open source content management system and it is a free content management system which can be used to build any type of website. Joomla is used as a content management system by small businesses and large organizations alike. WordPress is the easiest content management system and information on the WordPress website can be edited with a person with no knowledge of HTML. Ecommerce website is needed when a business sells something online and there are wide variety of ecommerce platforms including Magento, OsCommerce, and Open Cart. Magento is the perfect platform for newbie online sellers and it is search engine optimization ready too.

The website design should be able to fulfil the owner's website requirements and those who want to add blogs to the website can make use of dynamic websites. Flat design and responsive design continue to be the most popular trends in website designing. In responsive design, the layout of a website is going to be adjusted in response to different elements including width of the device. Prevalence of minimal navigation is another website designing trend influenced by mobile devices. Dynamic backgrounds are trendy in website designing and HTML 5 opens up new possibilities in website designing.

Visual storytelling is another prominent trend in the website designing landscape and photographs, icons and other visual elements are used in visual storytelling. The web has become less text heavy and it is expected that this trend will continue in the upcoming years too. Monochromatic is the leading trend in website designing colours and multicoloured approach goes hand in hand with new website designing trend. The major functional characteristics of a website get captured through the minimalist website designing pattern. The whole design in flat design is dependent on the hierarchy of design and the placing of elements on flat surfaces. One of the major features of flat design is the use of simple User Interface elements and the button and icons play a pivotal role in flat design.

It is ideal to select a website designing company that offers search engine optimization along with website designing. Having a unique website design is an important factor which helps us to distinguish ourselves from competitors. The web designing firm we choose should be professional to provide us with new ideas and concepts. Professional website design firms will be able to include unique functionality and design to promote products and services. Top rated website designing companies make use of the latest website development technologies.

Websites designed by a web designing company should be cross browser compatible as well as mobile responsive. An ideal website design firm creates a website that allows us to have complete access to content, images and pages. The latest trend in website designing is Cascading Style Sheets that don't need long codes for adding text, graphics and pictures in the website. CSS empowers website designers to create nice looking websites which has the right combination of text and pictorial elements. Eye catching, fascinating and simple designs characterise typical websites of contemporary age. Good content, proper spacing and usage of photographs form the essential elements of an elegant web design. Hiring a local website designer has many advantages and communication is important to the creation of a stunning website.

It is to be ensured that the website designers we select should have a stunning portfolio of website designs they have created. Top notch website designing companies offer the services of web hosting, content development and mobile websites. If a website designer provides web hosting, it will save clients from unforeseen costs of web hosting with little data space. A high quality website designer will be able to offer relevant mobile website options including Click to Call and location maps. Mobile compatible website design helps an enterprise to outrank their competitors and investing in a professional website designer will increase profits of the firm.

Custom website designers will have to create user friendly websites that enable visitors to easily navigate. Table less website designing is rapidly gaining momentum these days and every website designer of today use table less website designs for avoiding the complications. They are fast and quick in response when compared with websites designed using tables. A website designing specialist should be knowledgeable of colour schemes, themes, use of fonts, website structure and content. Well designed website is necessary to manage a successful online business venture today. The layout of the website is one of the most important elements of successful website designing.

Some companies prefer static website designing since it is cheaper as well as user friendly. Businesses which have just entered the market choose static website designing and it contains simple text and graphics. Static websites feature easy navigation, quick browsing and easy to download materials. The low pricing of static website designing attracts many companies and static website designing will become more dynamic if we seek help from a professional website designing company. Majority of the websites of today make use of WordPress platform and WordPress is the market leader in content management system.

A website designer ensures that page titles, page descriptions and headlines on the website are tweaked according to Search Engine Optimization requirements. The most talked about benefit of WordPress is that it is easy to use and the visual representation of a website is the key responsibility of a web designer. Website designers will be master experts in colour schemes, template design, and layout design. They use programs like Adobe Photoshop and Macromedia Fireworks to create stunning websites. Web development is often called the backend of the website and it refers to technical aspects of the website. The website functionality, navigation, and user experience fall under the broad umbrella of website development.

Flash Website Designing

The objective of flash technology is to generate animated designs on websites and flash plays a pivotal role in creating interactive websites. Flash website designing creates high impact on customers and traditional website designing is slowly getting replaced by flash website designing. Flash enables website designers to add movies and videos to the website that grabs the attention of website visitors. Corporate firms, education consultancies, retail stores and small businesses make use of the flash technology. Flash website designing is used to create animated websites with sound effects and clippings.

Website designers can reap rich benefits by incorporating flash technology in their websites and it is used for corporate presentations. Flash enhances the look of a typical website and it is designed according to the requirements of the user. It is utilized in professional websites for home page introduction, online demos and flash presentation of technical courses. Style and quality are the commendable features of a website created using the Flash technology. Flash Website Design Pro is a prominent HTML tool used for designing animated websites and flash banners. Website designers can design websites using Flash Website Design Pro within five minutes. Complex animations created using Flash website designing technology are elegant and eye catching.

Flash website designing permits a web designer to combine different fonts and effects within one animation. No Flash, HTML or programming skills are needed to use Flash Website Design Pro and it utilizes the latest website designing tools. Amazing Flash website designs won't have to bother about being distorted on different web browsers. They are compatible with all web browsers and the only thing required is installing a flash player in the computer. Website designers possessing creative skills of designing will excel in flash website designing.

Flash websites are more dynamic in nature when compared with traditional websites and they look appealing to the viewers. Flash website designs are used in the advertising of websites too and the content developed on Flash can be displayed using Adobe Flash Player. Easy updating of web content, search engine friendly web pages, easy integration with animation, and interactive features are the cherished attractions of flash website designing. Websites designed using Flash can be easily operated on Smartphones and flash website designing companies have specialized resources to deliver website with a splendid Flash banner. Flash also provides attractive gaming elements and dynamic 3D graphics along with resplendent animations. Flash websites of today are effective for better search engine optimization and marketing results.

More and more businesses are using Flash websites for creating fantastic and aesthetically pleasing websites. A powerful flash Content Management System (CMS) contains all essential instruments for creating an outstanding website. It should be mentioned that the features of flash website design shouldn't be overused and vector graphics images can be made with flash designs. The vector graphics employed by Flash features small file size and the ability to mix text, audio and graphics is the best feature of Flash websites. Flash makes the task of a marketer convenient to convey the message of a business in an interesting way.

An animated image, an integral part of Flash website designing, has the potential to convey the message of a business organization effectively. Sound effects created using Flash technology will offer captivating experience to the website visitor. Tutorials, online presentations, images, videos and movies can be made mesmerizing by using Flash technology. Majority of the elearning programs of today employ Flash website designing technology. The use of Flash reduces the usage of text in the website and websites created using Flash provide an extra graphical effect. A dull static website can be converted into a fantastic interactive website by using Flash. Flash intro in a site has become common today and flash website designing templates are highly popular among the website visitors.

Some of the successful flash website designing service companies offer the Flash 3D Unity development services. Some of the flash intros are interactive and many of them feature clippings about the company. Professional flash website designing is often found to be costly and website designers should ensure that flash website designs get good Search Engine Optimization rankings. As the URL (Uniform Resource Locator) of flash file is entered into the Google web crawler, it increases the SEO visibility of flash pages. Increasing number of organizations use Flash designs in their website mainly because of the numerous advantages it provides.

Flash website designing is most commonly used for designing intros, banners as well as text. Flash offers website designers a marvellous platform to express their creativity and aesthetic skills. The web pages created using Flash will be animated and it will be entirely different from a website created using HTML. Overloading the website with too many Flash designs will make the website loading time consuming. The usage of flash drives maximum web visitors to the site and a businessman can represent his company profile, product information and presentations in an attractive manner using Flash. According to website designing maestros, flash can be effectively used to embellish the design of a website.

Flash website designing should be performed in a unique way ensuring that it is not over done. Website designing experts point out that a successful website is a mixture of GIF images, HTML and Flash. Games produced in flash are extremely popular among users and flash websites created through animation produce better results. Plethora of online games are designed using Flash and they utilize AJAX (Asynchronous JavaScript and XML: web development technique) browser support. A website designer working with Flash can avoid the difficulties of XHTML design interfaces.

Flash can be used in devices such as CDs and flash movies are quite easy to download and store as small file. It has a user friendly interface which helps in solving complicated issues and the whole look of the website changes after Flash is used. Flash is essentially a static web designing technique for eye catching presentations and it can be used in different platforms including Smartphones. Professional looking websites can be easily created using Adobe Dreamweaver in less amount of time. Flash animations help a business to enhance their brand appeal and social networking websites use many features of Flash. Businesses of today are increasingly switching over to flash website designing tools and the advanced features in a flash website design need higher level of programming knowledge.

Joomla Website Designing

Joomla is a leading open source content management system and web developers prefer Joomla because it can be deployed in a short time frame. It is to be pointed out that large majority of Joomla's extensions and upgrades are available for free. Joomla website development tool satisfies the requirements of business owners, online merchants and retailers. The best feature of Joomla website development platform is its effective integration, processing and representation of data. The automated system of Joomla ensures that customer queries are answered in real time and Joomla helps to create SEO friendly web pages.

Joomla website development is affordable for any business and content in a Joomla site can be added, edited and deleted within no time. Joomla offers attractive designs and multiple language support is another top rated feature of Joomla. Joomla lets web designers to view pages in different languages with just one click and updating content in Joomla website takes only twenty or thirty minutes. Object oriented programming empowers Joomla to deliver content smoothly over the internet. The feel and look of a corporate website can be effectively managed by Joomla content management system. Joomla can be installed very easily and it is increasingly used by government organizations.

Joomla is the desired framework for making the website designing process incredible and it has great importance as an effective content management system. The website designing tool of Joomla is considered as the best tool for creating ecommerce, company and academic websites. Flexible website designing options are available in Joomla website designing system and Joomla designers emerge successful in creating stunning website designing patterns. Individuals with less technical knowledge too can use Joomla content management system and rich features of Joomla help it to stand out from the rest.

Joomla ensures reliable management of web content and easy to use admin feature is the top rated feature of Joomla. It has an "Article Manager" which lets to create and edit content in the website and the default article editor of Joomla is known as MCE Editor. Joomla has another content editor known as JCE and image management system in JCE allows uploading multiple images. Joomla is equipped with pre-existing modules and Joomla development modules can be created by the developers and made available to the public. This website designing tool is based on the PHP language which is compatible with search engines. Joomla can be used to make a highly functional ecommerce website and it is helpful in the easier integration of shopping cart modules and invoicing.

Multiuser authentication is another charismatic feature of Joomla and other prominent attractions of Joomla include banners, polls, RSS (Really Simple Syndication) and printable pages. Easy to change templates, multiple language support, search module integration, easy user management, and excellent photo gallery management made Joomla a stupendous hit among website designers. Personal websites, educational institution websites, corporate websites, and social networking sites can be made using the one and only Joomla. Joomla website design can increase the profitability of an online business and Joomla website designers will be able to convert webpage from Photoshop layout to CSS/HTML web page. Joomla framework is strong enough to check the security flaws as a content management system.

A Joomla website designer can offer many imaginative, amazing and interesting features to a website. Enhanced search abilities, infinite options to customize the web pages, and web based admin system make Joomla a favourite of website designers. There are more than 3800 extensions available in Joomla and they give a vibrant look to the web pages. Eye catching background colours and combination of font colours available in Joomla create collage of visual glory. Image, video, link, text, background, logo and theme in a Joomla based website look absolutely fascinating.

The introduction of Joomla as a content management system has simplified website designing and development. It has been pointed out that Joomla is user friendly for both developers and users and its free plug-ins enable users to add custom functionality. The built in SEO features of Joomla ensure that they get ranked well in the search engines. Options for email marketing and newsletters are available in Joomla, CMS with unlimited design options. The advantages of Joomla have made it on the forefront of the multibillion dollar web development industry.

Most of the Joomla website designs are customizable and it lets users to change fonts, colours as well as photos. Different aspects of Joomla website design include ecommerce, comments, news, reviews, calendar and property rental. Most of the Joomla website designing companies offer the services of Joomla customization, template design, Joomla maintenance, and Joomla ecommerce and extension development. Joomla has made website designing pleasurable, creative, aesthetic and a thing of joy forever. It is more popular than other HTML based website designing tools of contemporary period and installation, configuration, creation of content, creation of menus and modification of the site are the steps involved in Joomla website designing. The content hierarchy in Joomla is given below.

Section →Category→ Content item

Search engine friendliness, security, easy template integration, vast extension gallery, regular update, and community support are the top features of Joomla. Joomla is an open source content management system licensed under the GNU general public license. It makes use of an apache module called rewrite_module to generate search engine friendly URLs. Joomla enables its users to use custom page title, Meta description and Meta keyword in every page. Enhanced security is one of the attractive features of Joomla and the responsibility of Joomla security strike team is to find and fix security vulnerabilities.

Joomla has an incredible template integration system and any Joomla template can be integrated with few simple clicks. As Joomla Content Management System has Multilanguage support, it is popular among non English users too. There are three types of Joomla extensions including Component, Module as well as Plug-in. Joomla extensions can be found in the extension gallery of Joomla official site and regular updating of Joomla ensures security and reliability. Joomla has a big community on the internet and Joomla official support forum is one of the biggest in the world. It has a comprehensive documentation for website designers, web developers and site administrators on their site.

Mobile Website Designing

Mobile website design allows a user to access website using small screen mobile device like smartphone or tablet. They should be compatible with built in web browsers of Smartphones and it should offer a seamless browsing experience. Having a mobile website design has numerous advantages and it offers innumerable possibilities to enhance business. An aesthetically designed mobile website design has the potential to increase the number of visitors to a website. Mobile website design gives a professional look to websites and they target people who are constantly moving.

Buyers are more likely to buy products from a company which has a fully functional website on PC and mobile. Mobile websites of today are optimized so that they fit properly in the mobile screens and mobile website designing is entirely different from standard website designing. An ideal mobile website design should be accommodated in a small area and the visibility and brand value of mobile website should be enhanced. Most of the web development companies of today have added mobile website designing to their portfolio. Essential characteristics of mobile website design are speed, navigational difference, minimized text entry, and inbuilt functions. Speed is one of the most important aspects of mobile browsing and mobile website designers should take into account the aspect of speed.

According to top rung website designing experts, text entry for the mobile website needs to be reduced. Touch screen, non touch screen, or combinations of both contribute to the mobile website design of an enterprise. It has become increasingly important for businesses to invest in mobile website designing and mobile based websites are lighter than desktop based websites. If a visitor is able to jump from one page in mobile website to another easily, then the chances of turning visitors into customers increase. Mobile websites are search engine friendly and SEO friendly websites allow targeted audience to find websites very easily.

A completely responsive mobile website helps a company to stand out from their competitors. An ideal mobile website design should be hassle free and convenient for the website visitor or prospective customer. Using a mobile website is an easy way to promote new offers and information to potential customers. Incorporating a blog or newsfeed in mobile website will encourage users to return to the mobile website again and again. Simplicity is the key element of mobile website design and availability of whitespace is a recommended feature of mobile websites. The availability of WAP 2.0 and XHTML developers boost the growth of mobile website development.

As most Smartphones have a touch screen, mobile websites of today are designed with a touch interface. The size of the page should be taken into consideration before designing a mobile website. An ideal mobile website design should be accommodated in all mobile devices and mobile website strategy should be chalked out keeping in mind business needs. Mobile websites shouldn't contain lots of heavy data and good mobile website is a must requirement for improving the brand value of business. Mobile website designers should ensure that images load quickly and the text is automatically positioned to be readable on a smartphone.

Mobile website viewers navigate side by side whereas traditional website users move in a vertical pattern. This aspect should be kept in mind while designing a mobile website and mobile optimization will increase sales, generate more traffic and boost customer engagement. As mobile screens are small, mobile website designers will have to use the entire space available to bring the maximum impact. Smart website designers all over the length and breadth of the globe assign a simple style for mobile websites. It is recommended to use high resolution images in mobile website designing and graphics and images should be used in places where they are absolutely necessary.

The more attractive and simple to navigate a mobile website is, the more likely it is to be accessed by the customers. A mobile website should select a mobi domain instead of .com, .edu, .org etc which are meant for desktop browsing. Mobile websites should be tested on multiple platforms and mobile web surfers are looking for quick and responsive website. A mobile website development company should be well versed in hardware and software elements of mobile websites. Android, Symbian, Windows, iPhone and Blackberry platforms make use of mobile websites.

A perfect mobile website is one which runs on all platforms as well as operating systems. Mobile website designers will have a strong knowledge of mark up languages and proper testing of mobile websites is necessary. An ideal mobile website should have call to contact button, maps, driving directions and auto redirect to desktop website features. Since mobile website visitors need relevant information as quickly and as easily as possible, mobile websites need to be designed perfectly. Call to contact button in mobile website should be easy to find and the explosive growth of mobile internet points to the importance of a well designed mobile site. A business without a mobile optimized website will lose customers in the contemporary age of Information Technology.

The whole objective of a mobile website is to provide customers with an elegant user experience. An appealing, functional and responsive mobile website is a must for every businesses of today. Mobile website designers should ensure that customers are able to find what they are looking for with minimal effort. Social media links and legible text are two important components of mobile websites of any business. Mobile optimized websites get ranked well in search results and mobile friendly website design is a way to promote customer satisfaction and loyalty.

Majority of the mobile users will buy or use a service if the mobile website is very easy to navigate. Faster loading mobile website is generally preferred by customers and having a mobile website design requires fewer resources than an application. A mobile website plays a pivotal role in converting the users into customers and mobile website designers ensure that website designing is compatible with different screen resolutions. The design and appearance attract visitors to a mobile website and mobile sites should be made as simple as possible with minimum links. Mobile website design should be neat without too many links, photos, graphics as well as text. It is important to know the target audience before getting a mobile website designed and the requirements of target audience should be kept in mind.

How to Choose a Website Designing Company?

As website is one of the prominent marketing tools for an organization, the selection of website designing company has huge importance. A good website designing company should understand the objective behind having a stunning website. An ideal website designing company lays emphasis on the design aspect along with content aspect. Website designing companies of today utilize the latest technologies of HTML5 as well as CSS4. One of the important criteria while selecting a website designing company is that the company should follow latest website design technologies.

Each and every website created by a website designing company should be engaging and user friendly. Well known website designing companies take care of navigation system, website load time, content updating and search engine friendly design. People who want to utilize the services of a website designing company should check their past website designing projects. Top rated website designing companies maintain a blog on website designing and participate in various online website designing/development forums. Choosing the perfect website designing company is one of the most important decisions in business. A website designing company should have solid SEO (Search Engine Optimization) skills. Business owners should ensure that the style of websites created by a prospective website designing company matches their website.

The more experienced website designing companies are often the better performers and it is recommended not to choose companies with less than five years of experience. One of the best ways to select a top notch website designing company is by comparing companies that can be found online. When creating a deal with a website designing company, everything should be written in records. Businesses opting for the services of website designing companies should check whether websites created by them are appealing and whether they grab attention. They should ask the website design company for references and prospective seekers of website designing company should know the following things.

What is the purpose of the website?

Is it an informational site?

Does it sell products or services?

Do you want visitors of your site to interact?

Do you want visitors to download a file?

Do you want visitors to click on ads?

Knowing what type of website we will need help us to select the services of a website designing company. Website designing companies with an illustrious track record design informational sites, ecommerce sites and portfolio sites. Some website designing companies specialize in specific categories of websites and business owners looking for the services of a website designing company should have a crystal clear idea about their content updating requirements.

A website designing company should understand the content requirements of various online directories. Picture layout, website design navigation, budget and impressive Flash effects determine the suitability of a website designing company. Business owners should ask the representatives of website designing companies to show the clause in contract where website ownership is mentioned. Clients should get file backup from the website designing company in CD and they should necessarily get the FTP (File Transfer Protocol) login URL, user name, and password. It is best to register domain name in a company like GoDaddy.com and getting an understanding of the costs involved in website designing is important.

It is desirable to sign long term contract with a website designing company as it will benefit both the company and the client. Some website designing companies charge ongoing maintenance fee and the agreement should explicitly state who will create the content in website. Project managers of the client organizations should ensure that the delivery date of the website designing company works for them. The customers of a well known website designing company will be extremely happy with the results and checking online reviews is recommended. A well built and efficient website marks the credibility of a website designing company in a seamless way.

Having a content management system that is data driven is important and it ensures that the website is searchable and flexible. An ideal content management system offered by a website designing company should allow us to alter page titles, Meta description and keywords. Although flash based websites look amazingly aesthetic, they are difficult to get indexed in search engines. It is advisable to avoid Flash based websites since increasing number of netizens are using mobile internet. Websites designed by an efficient website designing company will be scalable as well as future proof.

Ecommerce and mailing list systems are integrated in a website designing package offered by prominent companies. Before selecting a website designing company, a client should ask the following questions.

Are the designs clear and aesthetic?

Does the design possess a professional appearance?

Is the navigation easy to use?

Is their grammar, spelling and language usage correct?

It is important to know how flexible, responsive and knowledgeable a website designing company or an independent website designer is. Clients are keen on looking through the portfolio of website designing companies and they prefer professional and easy to use websites. An ideal website design for a company should match with their products or service offering seamlessly.

It is necessary to check the knowledge base of a website designing company before selecting their services. They should be up to date with latest search engine optimization strategies and web 2.0 marketing techniques. A website designing company should be able to offer high quality internet marketing campaign for their clients. While selecting a website designing company, clients should keep in mind that good website brings in more customers while a bad website drives away prospective customers. Websites created by an elegant website designing company should have a unique feel and they will allow us to contact their previous clients.

Well known website designing companies will have structured planning as well as implementation processes. Some website designing companies offer blog setup as a part of their website designing packages and such companies definitely carry a brownie point. Clients should have a crystal clear idea about who owns the intellectual property rights to the final website. Prospective clients should ask website designing companies the questions of "will they maintain website after initial design"? " do they offer hourly rate or fixed project payment?", and "how much payment should be made upfront?" As a general rule of thumb, a well crafted 10 page website will cost an average rate of $3000.

Search Engine Optimization and Website Designing

The aspect of search engine optimization should be taken into account while designing a website. There are three elements to successful search engine optimization: keyword selection, on page factors and off page factors. Fine keyword selection refers to identifying the words and phrases prospective buyers are searching for. Finding the right combination between search volume and competition is extremely important in SEO. Content and site structure forms the crux of on page search ranking factors and keywords should be carefully used in content.

Creating content for human visitors has become an essential Search Engine Optimization strategy of today. Other on page SEO factors include the use of text links on the page, file name and Uniform Resource Locator (URL) names. Ignoring the importance of search engine optimization in website designing will be a huge mistake. Making a website search engine friendly is a continuous process and it is equally important just like the website designing. SEO measures should be taken right at the time of website designing itself and designing SEO friendly website is not that much difficult as many of us may think. The first step in SEO friendly website designing begins with HTML coding and SEO friendly HTML coding helps search engine crawlers to crawl the website easily.

A good website design should be one which can draw traffic to a website and generate revenue for the business. An ideal website design should have SEO guidelines included in it and SEO website designing refers to adherence to all the on page SEO factors. A website designer should use keyword rich URLs while designing the website in order to rank effectively in search engines. Over usage of multimedia or graphics is not recommended in a search engine optimized website. Titles, Meta descriptions, and header tags should be used for all pages in order to clearly define what the web page is about.

Adding proper ALT tags for images is important since it tells search engines what the image is about. SEO conscious website designers create detailed HTML sitemap as an effective search engine optimization strategy. Following the SEO guidelines lead to better indexing of website, increased visitor traffic and improved conversion rates. Creating content rich website is essential from the SEO viewpoint and web pages need proper visibility. Website designers/developers will have to focus exclusively on driving massive traffic online using website designing, search engine marketing, directory submission, analytics and social media optimization. Search Engine Optimization and website designing should go hand in hand and search engine optimization forms a major component of website designing.

The services of Search Engine Optimization consultant are needed before the website is created. Web page architecture should be created keeping in mind what the target audience seeks online. Website developers seek advice from SEO specialist while creating navigation schemes, categories, headings, and breadcrumb links. The process of Search Engine Optimization starts with the planning and designing of a website. Creation of robots.txt file, HTML and XML sitemap are important steps in on-page search engine optimization.

If a website is designed in such a way that it supports all SEO features, then the chances of getting higher search engine rankings are more. Optimizing the benefits of a well designed website will result in more traffic and the most common design mistakes from a SEO viewpoint are making website completely in Flash, adding images without ALT tags, and nonexistent title tag. Although Flash and image can be used to enhance the look and feel of a website, the site must have text to build relevance for major search engines including Google, Yahoo and Bing. The balance between search engine optimization and website designing determines the success of a website in traffic generation. Search engine optimization is incomplete without good website design and it needs to be built into the website designing process.

Businesses don't often think about Search Engine Optimization before a website is designed and these websites lack SEO features. SEO is an integral part of website designing or redesigning process and website SEO is fundamental for online businesses to succeed. A SEO friendly site is one that allows search engines to explore pages across the site and search engines should be able to easily crawl through a website in order to ensure higher SEO rankings. Not all website designing technologies are built keeping in mind the art and science of Search Engine Optimization. Building SEO friendly website needs careful planning as well as meticulous approach from the website designer/website developer.

A website should be made on a crystal clear internet marketing plan with focused approach and value proposition. All variations and sub domains of SEO friendly website should point to the main site and it is extremely important. The web hosting of SEO friendly website should be fast as well as platform specific and WP Engine is a fantastic example (It offers a platform tailored to WordPress websites). The Content Management System we choose influence Search Engine Optimization and WordPress is the best option available today. An ideal Content Management System should correspond to the business needs of an organization.

The main content of a website should be text based so that search engines can easily crawl the website. Images, content, videos and PDFs are sources of search engine traffic and the only requirement is that they should be easily discoverable. Primary navigation and XML sitemaps help search engines crawl the website and discover new pages. Things should be organized in a SEO friendly site in such a way that it simplifies navigation. Sensible naming convention is essential for a URL to get ranked well in search engines and sites optimized for search engines should give equal consideration to the mobile layouts.

Website designers should think of the needs and wants of mobile users and mobile friendliness is a ranking factor for mobile search. Another important consideration in mobile friendly design is the page speed and Google's mobile friendly test tool will give feedback on mobile friendliness of a site. Web usability is a combination of device design, page speed, website design convention and innovative approach to website designing keeping the website visitor in mind. Page layout, visual hierarchy, site navigation, site search, and design should be considered in our endeavour to make site SEO friendly. Content and SEO combination is an essential requirement of search engine friendly website designing.

Website Designing Ideas for Small Business

Website designing has great impact on small businesses and companies specializing in website designing for small businesses can give a great insight into how designing affects customer behaviour. An ideal small website design company offers value to customers and the information available in a small business website should be easy to find. Search box is an important tool for website visitors and Flash website design offers lots of navigation options. The website of a small business should include company name and description of the services. The "Contact Us" page of a small business website should include several ways to contact our business.

Including an email form on the website is important and small businesses can benefit from the inclusion of social media elements in their website design. Visitors should be able to share site's information with their Twitter and Facebook accounts. Website design ideas for small business create a pivotal role in creating an impression about the website. The elements of website designing for small businesses are determined by the answers to the following questions.

What information will the website provide to visitors?

Do we need a shopping cart in our website to allow online purchases?

Is it necessary to incorporate a blog into the website?

It is always best to choose a company that offers both the services of search engine optimization and website designing. Outsourcing the website designing has become very popular now and it helps client companies to save money. A better web presence is necessary for a small business and getting in touch with the right website design company is important. The theme and purpose of the website should be very clear to the website visitor and some website designers add elegant graphics to spice up website design. Supplying contact details in the website of a small website is absolutely important and giving freebies to potential customers is an innovative idea.

Restricting the number of advertisements is another important website design tip and audio loading, scrolling texts and animated GIFs should be avoided in a website. Avoiding popup windows in a website is recommended and clients will navigate away from the website if there are lots of ads on the website. Experienced website designers create shortcuts to specific sites and careful observation of best website design ideas will be helpful in retaining regular traffic. According to seasoned website designers, an ideal website design should be unique, creative as well as responsive. The contents in a typical website should be presented in an attractive and simple manner.

Ideas for the website design will help us to create a super splendid website and swap images can be used in a typical website. Designing swap images is funny and rollover images add an element of elegance to the website. Rollover images are extremely popular with web designers who are passionate about playing with new designs. DHTML (Dynamic Hypertext Mark up Language) is highly useful for complex navigation systems. Insertion of Flash animation will make the website really fantastic and eye catching graphics is a vital element of website design.

It is recommended to use smart tables in the website in order to make it look attractive and aesthetic. Fast loading website designs are recommended by website designers and websites should be suitable for all resolutions. An ideal website is browser compatible and it works well in all web browsers and professional fonts should be used in a website. Splendid colours should be used in a website since they are considered as thing of attraction forever. Website designers should not clutter web page with unnecessary images as well as graphics. Large images shouldn't be used in an aesthetically designed website and website designers should leave lots of whitespace in a website.

Website designers should check for broken links before uploading the site and some of the elegant WordPress themes are Selecta, Librio, Black Power and Compositio. An average web user was impressed with just one Photoshop image earlier and the scenario has been changed completely now. Inserting QR code is a great way to attract new visitors to a website and new standards are being used instead of the content created using Adobe Flash. Using a beautiful image as background is an important aspect of great website design and the image should be relevant to content. Cut-down colour pattern on a website makes it absolutely stunning and using different shades of main colours help the design to stand out.

Parallax scrolling and depth perception in a website design ensures that the site works well in three dimensions. The innovative usage of colour schemes, logos, texts and links will make a website design amazing. Viewer experience should be kept in mind before selecting a website design and the old adage "First impression is the best impression" is relevant for website designs too. The overall look and feel of a typical website is very important and it increases the number of visitors to the website.

Website designers should ensure that the logo is in the upper front corner of each page along with a tagline. Building an ecommerce site is different from building a website for other purposes and it is better to have a specific product niche in mind for the website. Website designers use simple business templates for designing an electronic commerce website. A typical ecommerce site should be as simple as possible and it requires high sense of creativity to create stunning websites. A rich website design acts as a catalyst to the business development initiatives of an organization.

Selection of technologies makes a huge impact on website design and AJAX, PHP and Flash are the most popular website designing technologies. A beautiful website will create an everlasting impression and it will attract visitors again and again. The photographs in a typical business website should be impressive and attractive to the website visitor. The website content should be easy to navigate and a feature called key press navigation helps visitors to navigate all around the site by using their keyboard. The usage of different sized fonts and magazine style layouts has become common in website designing of contemporary age. There will be little difference between the web and print content in the upcoming days of creative website designing.

Responsive Website Designing

Responsive website designing is needed to enable web pages to look good on all types of devices. It is aimed at coding a website to give an optimal viewing, reading experience, navigation experience and scrolling across different devices. A website designer should ensure that website's images, text, layouts, and navigation elements should be able to readjust on a wide variety of devices. Making a responsive website will cost more than a conventional website and responsive website design reduces the total cost of ownership. It removes the effort to maintain various versions of particular website, such as desktop version and mobile version.

According to eminent website designers, investing in responsive design is a smart decision and long term technology solution. The standard responsive website design will be "one size, fits all devices" and responsive website design is about offering an optimal user experience. Responsive website design is not tied to particular devices and it offers best experience on a website. The responsive website design has become popular with the advent of smart phones and iPad. Responsive website designing uses a fluid design process and it involves prototyping, sketching and view framing. Website designers of today rely on wire framing, quick sketches and CSS and HTML prototypes.

Skilled website designers of today concentrate on designing more elements and fewer layouts. HTML should be used as early as possible in website designing and it is an innovative idea to create wireframes which can be moved easily. Choosing the type of navigation in a website should be based on the information along with design considerations. The navigation of a website should be tested on as many devices as possible and responsive website designs are developed to respond to different platforms like Smartphones, tablets and Kindles. A website designed using responsive website designing approach works on most devices and a responsive website will adapt to the size of the browser being used.

Few of the shopping facilities of an ecommerce website include user friendly ecommerce websites, active social media engagement and mobile payment systems. Responsive website design bridges the usage gap between personal computers and mobile devices. A responsive website design is necessary to succeed in online business and designing responsive websites is about designing websites that are user friendly. Picture scaling can be accomplished by utilizing CSS with extreme pixel width for all pictures contained on the page. Almost all web browsers of today support picture scaling and Google loves and favours responsive website designs.

Responsive website design maintains the same look and feel of a website irrespective of devices. The responsive website design takes care of factors such as screen size, pixel resolution as well as click versus touch. Responsive website design takes care of search Engine Optimization and Google likes responsive websites. While moving to a responsive website design, we can maintain all back links the original site has. Responsive website combats the problem of reduction in bounce rates by presenting all of the same content found on the desktop website.

Responsive website design reduces time for loading and it improves mobile search rankings. As mobile searches have surpassed web searches, Google ranks URLs optimized for mobile higher in rank. Responsive website design is the best for mobile search and responsive website design enhances user experience. A responsive website design will keep all social shares to a single site and it is cost effective when compared to building a mobile website. Responsive website design is quite instrumental in bringing good reputation to the company. Growing number of websites are adopting responsive website design and design part will never interfere with usability. A responsively designed website will never have issues with links, texts, images and scrolling.

Responsive website design guarantees higher rankings and superior visibility on Google and it brings more offline browsing experience. The responsive website design ensures that the website gains the ability to never look outdated. Businesses of today can't ignore the benefits of responsive website design and responsive website design services can dynamically change a website's appearance depending upon the used device's screen. In responsive website designing, all devices are served by the same HTML with the use of CSS which decides the web page's layout. Instead of building up separate websites for tablets, phones, desktops, laptops and big screen monitors, the users are supported by single code.

List of responsive website designing services include designing responsive website layouts, developing unique slide shows, building mobile friendly systems, designing unique artworks and designing personalized website features. Responsive website design is necessary for the development of a website and it is the technology of the future. Responsive website designing ensures that we don't have to worry about the content parity. Having a responsive website design can keep our site on the top of technology changes and it has paved the way towards the end of designing sites for fixed viewports. Responsive website design is user first, context first, mobile first and platform independent.

Responsive website design can dramatically increase sales and a business without responsive website design is underperforming. Responsive website designs are sites that quickly adapt to the screen size of the device. Special coding techniques are utilized in a responsive website and sites with responsive design look great on desktops and laptops. Responsive website designers should understand that website is a great tool for branding and generating sales. Businesses that provide seamless online experience across all platforms will be able to generate more engagement and more sales.

Responsive website design takes the same basic elements across all platforms and proportion based grids ensure that websites will be optimized to deliver. It is the modern approach to designing quality websites and this design reacts instantly to any changes. The key components of responsive website design are flexible grids, flexible media and media queries. The first and foremost website layout requirement is to have a fluctuating grid foundation. Media queries come in handy when the designers target and include different website layout styles. Media query can be combined with flexible grids and flexible media that will pave the way towards responsive website design. Different elements of responsive website design include navigation, columns, call to action, branding and whitespace.

Animation as a Tool for Interactive Website Designing.

Animation acts as an important tool for website designers and it has similar importance along with graphic and visual options. Animation has become an inseparable element of user interface design and it plays an important role in attracting visitors. It acts as a guide for visitors to delve deeper into the web pages and improve usability of the website content. Both Flash and frame based animation are used in website design and too much Flash content in a website should be avoided. The user interface gets better in terms of its performance across multiple browsers as well as devices.

Animation is of great importance in setting the tone of the user interface and it helps in guiding the user and enhancing user experience. Animation has the unlimited potential to give real experience in virtual setting through excellent designs. Introducing surprise elements in menu icons of animation alters and enhances the user experience. Animation can be effectively used as a mechanism to obtain feedback from users and it is often used as an interactive tool. CSS3 and jQuery enable easy animation of items on pages and the products page should have enhanced visual size. Product or service menu should have a promo which catches the user's attention including "register now", "free sign up" and "Request for Quote".

Small promos in animation can be used as a guidance tool to comprehend what the website is all about. Enchanting animation should be the focus of every website designer and website designers are passionate about providing a great user interface. The animation should satisfy some goals including task performance, enhanced speed of operation, creating synergy between the user and business goal. CSS3 supports master techniques of animation and enhanced usage of animation can be utilized for interactive website designing. Animation should not be ignored in the website designing process and animation refers to quick display of an image sequence.

Animation can be created by making slight changes in image and animation slices become cells in HTML table. Photoshop Extended and Apple QuickTime application can be used to play video. Images taken using digital camera should be tweaked using Adobe Bridge and Camera Raw Dialog box. Any type of graphics image can be converted to dazzling animation and an individual image used in animation is called as frame. Animation combines the usage of colour, film language and sound. 3D animation has scaled new heights of popularity and 2D animation plays an important role in animation. Efficiency, simplicity, and cost effectiveness are the advantages of two dimensional animations.

One of the best benefits of animation is efficiency and it needs great amount of creativity to produce remarkable animation. Designs provided by 2D animation are less complex than designs provided by 3D animation. Action movies benefit immensely from 3D animation and detailed action and complex images are the features of 3D animation. Some television shows have created their success saga on 2D animation and educational applications make use of 3D animation. The efficiency and simplicity of 2D animation leads to greater cost effectiveness and 2D animation takes less time.

Small companies increasingly make use of 2D animation and the creative possibilities offered by 2D animation are endless. Traditional animation lets website designers to create animated cartoons and animated projects. 2D animation lets us to easily create images and it requires higher level of talent when compared with 3D animation. Concept design, character design and storyboard development are steps involved in the creation of animation development. Two dimensional animation is associated with shape, colour, transparency, structure as well as texture. The power of computer technology has made the animation very simple and the field of computer animation is a subset of computer graphics. Animation is achieved through a series of geometric transformations, translation, rotation and any mathematical technique to produce sequence of scenes.

All cartoon characters are the creation of wonderful animation art and basic animation is effective and simple. Animation adds life to a website or movie and internet users are fond of browsing a graphics rich website. Website designers can't design a website without basic animation and basic animation is the illusion of different movements linked in an appropriate way. The three basic types of animation are cel animation, stop animation and computer animation. Cel animation is the traditional way of animating a series of hand drawings and different images are created in the process of animation.

The transparent sheet in an animation is known as cel and it is an effective technique that saves time by combining shapes as well as origins. Stop motion animation is an animation technique to make objects move on their own. Computer animation is the latest animation technique which consists of two dimensional animation and three dimensional animation. 2D animation is generally used by PowerPoint and Flash animations and they improve design of the characters. 2D animation possesses some similarities with cel animation and it has become very popular due to the simple application drawings. The three basic types of animation have brought a new era of innovation in website design, computer graphics, film and media.

Cel animation can be drawn more attractive by using drawings, music, sound effects and Toon Boom Studio 4 is a top rated two dimensional animation software program. It is an application made by animators for animators and Toon Boom Studio 4 can be used to create stunning animations. Animationish is a fantastic program for learning the basics of animations and Flip Boom is animation software intended for children. The control output of Flip Boom has been reduced to make this software as simple as possible. Adobe Flash is easy to use and the software After Effects is used for compositing and effects.

Pencil is a top notch animation program that allows both vector and bitmap drawings and Photoshop drawings are often incorporated into Flash. The software has been reduced to provide essential elements and it serves as an excellent introduction to animation software. Synfig is rated as fantastic animation software and it can create complex lighting as well as camera effects. The animation software Crea Toon is almost similar to animation software Toon Boom and it is less refined animation software. Toon Boom Digital Pro is for experienced animators and some of the most successful animators make use of this software.

Ecommerce Website Designing

Ecommerce website designing is a little bit different from conventional website designing and they feature dynamic website designs. An ideal Electronic commerce website should be attractive, responsive, as well as customized. Ecommerce website design should be unique, attractive, stylish, professional, and beautiful. Gracefully designed ecommerce website attracts visitors and website designers try to make an Ecommerce site enticing. An ecommerce site should be designed in such a way that visitors want to visit the site again and again.

Addition of design elements, plug-ins, widgets and animation beautify an ecommerce website. An ideal ecommerce site should be search engine friendly, user friendly as well as marvellous. Website designers should focus on creating search engine friendly electronic commerce websites. Ecommerce website should appear at the top of search engine results and the pages of an ecommerce website should work with enhanced needs of the user. Multimedia files are embedded to create stylish look and multimedia file such as Flash should be avoided in an ecommerce website. As majority of the search engines don't acknowledge Flash technology, it is recommended to avoid them in an ecommerce site. Quality content is an essential feature of ecommerce website and software that creates templates for any kind of site is called as theme generator.

Ecommerce website design has taken the lead in the online world and ecommerce website designing takes care of the designing needs of ecommerce websites. Electronic commerce websites are specially designed to encourage visitors to buy products. Business relevant look and feel reflects a typical ecommerce website and organized layout and professional design characterise a typical ecommerce website. An ecommerce site should include proper navigation, market friendly content, customer friendly user interface and simple checkout. Ecommerce sites are integrated with professional payment gateway to ensure smooth and hassle free online payment system.

Professional and talented ecommerce website designers design an ecommerce website that will eventually become a success. It is important to hire an experienced ecommerce website designer and an ecommerce site is in the safe hands of ecommerce website designer. Any professional ecommerce website designer will have several successful projects to his credit. An ideal ecommerce website designer will have exposure to all elements of ecommerce website designing and some professional ecommerce website designers work independently. An ecommerce site will have the ability to draw customers and deliver significant conversion rates. Talent and professionalism are two essential traits of electronic commerce website designers. The aim of a website designer should be to deliver an ecommerce site that delivers requisite Return on Investment.

The duties of an ecommerce website designer are conceptualization and integration with the payment gateway. The buying experience in an ecommerce site should be smooth and clients should choose an ecommerce website designer who understands the responsibilities of designing an ecommerce store. Complete set of skills and an aptitude for design punctuate a typical ecommerce website designer. An ecommerce website designer should be conversant with market trends and they should consider preferences and professional standards of target audience. Buyers are more willing to buy products from sites with clean as well as professional design.

There are many ecommerce solutions available in the market including OsCommerce, Magento, Virtue Mart and Open Cart. Open Cart is an ecommerce shopping cart solution and it is an open source software solution. An ecommerce website designer ensures that a website of a business is well designed and an ecommerce site is geared towards promoting a business's visibility. Collecting payment from the customer, calculating refunds, shipping and handling refunds are critical elements in an ecommerce website. An ecommerce site requires an online shopping cart program that helps customers to purchase together for checkout. The ecommerce website should have a comprehensive product page and site design should convey a sense of professionalism.

The need for high quality ecommerce website design has become a priority and it is to be ensured that an ecommerce site keeps ahead of the competition. A website designing company or a freelance website designer should understand specific challenges of the ecommerce project. An ecommerce site should be easy for customers to purchase and find whatever product they need. An easy and enjoyable shopping experience characterises a typical electronic commerce website. A high quality ecommerce design company will take the niche needs of business into consideration before designing website.

It is quite important to direct customers to a clear path to purchase products and services in an ecommerce website. An ecommerce site should make pricing information visible and it should highlight any discounts available in a crystal clear manner. Flash technology can be used in an ecommerce site to create special effects and it allows one to add animation and videos to a web page. Beautification of the website is the primary objective of an ecommerce website and an ecommerce website design company tries to make the website as appealing as possible. Visual impact is the primary focus of an ecommerce website design and Flash is of extreme help in presenting complex content in a simple manner.

As Flash is not a search engine friendly technology, some ecommerce sites avoid its usage and Google has started indexing some Flash files. The designing of ecommerce sites will cost more when compared with traditional websites and the time spent on setting up an ecommerce site is an investment. An ecommerce site should look absolutely professional and layout and easy to use navigation are the essential features of an excellent ecommerce website. According to ecommerce maestros, ideal ecommerce site should be clear, concise as well as benefits focused. Solid marketing strategy forms the basis of a successful ecommerce website and thinking about the customers of a business is really important.

An ecommerce site should strategically position their products and a "Continue Shopping" feature should be installed in an ecommerce site. Great and user friendly customer experience is expected in an ecommerce website and some of them cross sell other products by suggesting other items. Another important ecommerce website design tip is to provide an option to checkout as a guest. Network security experts suggest using a recognizable Secure Sockets Layer in an ecommerce site. A website designer needs to consider variety of online selling principles while designing an ecommerce site.

WordPress Website Designing Service

WordPress is an excellent website design program and WordPress separates different elements of website design including page content, website look and website functionality. Page content is the important part of any website designing service and the WordPress installation gives websites some functionality. WordPress offers extensions to improve and modify the functionality of a website and variety of different SEO plug-ins offer control over basic website design. None of the content management systems can beat the WordPress and WordPress is a versatile CMS. Different benefits of WordPress website designing service include effective content distribution, variety of plug-in, large collection of themes, low cost and intra site linking.

WordPress works like a content distribution engine when it is setup properly and it boosts website's search engine rankings. WordPress website can be configured to distribute the website content in social media sites and RSS aggregator sites. All WordPress plug-ins are completely free and hundreds of WordPress themes are available for website design. All WordPress themes are highly customizable and they are available in one column, two column, three column and open formats. Businesses should buy a custom URL and contact hosting service provider to get affordable hosting solutions. Intra site linking is absolutely essential for usability and search engine optimization and web pages can be used to link web pages through menus, tags and archives.

WordPress CMS has evolved into high end content management system and blogging platform. The possibilities offered by WordPress are limitless and the purpose of WordPress is to express ideas and add content that makes users coming back. The initial quality of WordPress should be impeccable and HTML or CSS will load faster on slow connections. If the WordPress content relies on user interaction, it is better to use PHP (Hypertext Preprocessor) or My SQL. A website should be designed in such a way that it works on any operating system and WordPress is all about sharing ideas.

It is desirable to employ a WordPress specialized website designer and WordPress is a newbie friendly website designing tool. WordPress offers easily navigable content management system that aids in designing a website in an easy manner. User friendly features of WordPress make it highly popular among aesthetic website designers. The websites created on WordPress website design platform are compatible with almost all web browsers. The SEO objective of website can be easily achieved using WordPress content management system. WordPress website designing is cost effective and WordPress website designers are provided with an opportunity to customize WordPress using various themes. The simple programming language of WordPress makes it compatible with search engines.

There is no need of having programming or coding knowledge to use WordPress and the owners can easily make changes in the website. Fresh and appealing look to website is the charismatic attraction of websites designed using WordPress. WordPress has become an interface of choice for websites to create stunning customized websites. Availability of diverse plug-ins allows added functionality to a website and five essential WordPress plug-ins are Yoast, WordPress Google Analytics, Contact Form 7, Flamingo and W3 Total Cache. Yoast allows easy creation of website sitemap, editing of robots.txt, Meta description and image attribute.

The functionalities of WordPress Google Analytics are monitoring the WordPress website, analyzing visitor of the website page, and showing the statistics on the blog itself. The integration of Google Analytics and Google AdSense allow monitoring and improving the website performance. Contact Form 7 allows creation of contact forms for website visitors and it allows receiving queries from visitors. Flamingo allows the messages submitted through Contact form to be easily saved into a database. Easy recording and retrieval of visitor's message is the specialty of Flamingo and W3 Total Cache allows improving website user experience. WordPress is fully compatible with W3C standards and effective and visually attractive website is the end result of WordPress.

WordPress comes with a web design brand and it displays fantastically on a mobile device. The premium types of WordPress themes cost between $25-$120 and hundreds of plug-ins, tools and libraries are the special features of WordPress. Ten million websites across the globe make use of WordPress and responsive design has become a defacto standard in website designing. Video headers are becoming a popular tool to narrate the story in website designing and parallax creates 3D illusion by making the background move at a slower pace. WordPress development companies include parallax effect in the one page website and parallax will become the favourite of website designers in 2018.

Cards enable the website content segregation into multiple sections and the excellent textual representation has become a mainstay of the web development world. Flat colours will become thing of the past in website designing and WordPress has an intuitive website UI design. Adding blog pages, new pages, images, and other elements can be performed in WordPress with ease. Teams can easily collaborate on WordPress projects and a WordPress website can add other features of video gallery, Facebook Fan Box, Twitter feed as well as event calendar. Many prestigious organizations utilize WordPress platform and WordPress platform is flexible for online business.

WordPress is one of the most commonly used content management systems in the world and fast installation process is the first and foremost quality of a WordPress website. The automatic installation system of WordPress allows it to install within five minutes and WordPress is great for small businesses as it is free of cost. WordPress is extremely user friendly and there are a number of default themes installed in WordPress. Different number of plug-ins available in WordPress will be able to extend the functionality. Ability to paginate the blog posts is another peculiar feature of WordPress content management system.

WordPress follows all the web standards and WordPress is absolutely search engine optimization friendly. The tagging of posts, sending of pings to other sites and the use of H1/H2 tags are the SEO functionalities embedded in WordPress. WordPress themes enable us to customize the header and the header is really an important element in the design of website. The side bars of WordPress website are customizable and there are specific colours connected with various niches. Widgets in WordPress are helpful for placing banners and the majority of WordPress plug-ins are coded in PHP scripting language. Built in SEO features of WordPress are often pointed out as the impeccable feature of the content management system.

Website Designing Best Practices

Paragraphs in a website should be more than five or six sentences long and it is ideal to divide long paragraphs into two or three paragraphs. Creating Cascading Style Sheet for website is recommended and it helps us to save lots of time. The usage of simple and straightforward menus is recommended as a best website designing strategy. Menus in a website should be easy to understand and the usage of Flash is not at all recommended in a website. Website designers should not add too much JavaScript to the website and too much JavaScript will reduce the speed of the website.

JavaScript is not compatible with all web browsers and we may lose visitors if we include too much JavaScript in the website. Adding too much pictures in a website is not at all recommended and it is another important website designing best practice. The speed of the website will be reduced if we add too much pictures to our website and Photoshop or any other image editing software can be used to reduce the size of an image file. We should use three or more different colours in the website and the colour of the text should be different from the background colour.

An ideal website should be fully functional and all internal and external hyperlinks should work. A website should be compatible with W3C standards and it should work with all web browsers including Internet Explorer, Firefox, Chrome and Safari. Websites should work properly on all mobile devices and good website design will help us to grow business. Using clear and quick navigation in a website design is absolutely important and it is recommended to start by placing site's title at the top of the page. Linking category and sub category pages is recommended and keeping links in blue is not a hard and fast rule.

Minimizing animation and flashing banners in a website is recommended by website designing experts. Having an "about me" page gives them a personal glimpse into who we are and a well written "about me" page will create credibility. A commercial website is the virtual business residence and it is important to practice good website design principles to ensure that site is successful. The most important principle of website design is an understanding of different components to use in the website. A website page layout is one of the most important aspects of a website and web page layout is a part of website design.

The first priority of a website designer is to create a website that does not load slowly and there seems to be a relationship between aesthetic level and functionality. It is suggested to keep the number of images on a page to minimum and images make up for a large percentage of a website's download speed. Although images enhance a page's visual quality, the phrase "less is more" still holds true for most cases. Images we use in a website should be of the formats JPEG, GIF or PNG format and JPEG should be selected for images with full colours. It is recommended that GIF and PNG are good for flat colour images including logos, buttons, and cartoons.

The resolution of website images should be set to 72 DPI (Dots per Inches) and tables are great for presenting tabular data. The usage of animated GIFs should be avoided unless it is absolutely necessary and the page size should be kept under 30 KB. The page weight consists of page's text, images, and media components including sound and video. A talented website designer strikes a balance between the aesthetic qualities of a website and loading speed. Website designing companies of today say that they will have to design websites for Internet Explorer, Mozilla Firefox, Apple's Safari, Opera and Google Chrome.

Small business website design cost has increased in the recent years and a website should be designed in such a way that it looks appealing. The header, logo and navigation areas in a website should not be changed from one page to another. The text, pictures and spaces in a website should possess a fine balance and the content should be presented in an illustrative manner. Content in a website should be presented with headings, sub headings, comma and with colour elaborations. Different colours should be used in the text at different levels and the keyword should be used repeatedly.

Offering several payment options from trusted names such as PayPal, Google and Sage Pay will add an element of credibility in the design of an ecommerce site. Coding HTML and CSS will always be part of the web design skill set and keeping the CSS code organized is the first step towards writing elegant code. Every element in CSS style sheet should be semantically written and organized and a coherent structure should be used in CSS coding. Visitors should always know which page they are on and if a website doesn't load in 12 seconds, statistics show that 43% of visitors will leave the site. According to website designing aficionados, there are two main parts of a website: images/graphics as well as content.

The design strategy should remain in the minds of website designers while conceptualizing the navigation in a website. Clear and simple layout helps us to easily navigate and find what we are looking for very easily. The content in a website should be clear and to the point and making use of "Call to Actions" is important. Features such as polls, comment boxes, video tutorials, links and online games are rich user interface applications. The usage of large images in a website should be discouraged and it is ideal to keep multimedia elements in minimum.

We shouldn't use background music, banners or animations that appear while visitors read our content. Although multimedia content is great for website, the excessive usage of multimedia content should be avoided. Logos, colour palette, and navigation buttons contribute to the unity of the website design. Easy navigation is linked to the content design and a clear title should be followed by clear text. Website design denotes the overall quality of a website and web page standardization, web page layout, web page width, page background and use of fonts should be taken into consideration while designing a website. It is important to keep the background colour of the pages, tables, lists and panels same for each page.

Improving Website Designing

Website designers should ensure that web pages don't have visual related clutter on them and the "fold" is always visible to the online audience. The "fold" refers to the part of the web page which is visible without scrolling and it is very important that the website should be mobile friendly. An ideal website design should be viewable in any type of electronic gadget and the viewer should have optimal user experience. Using standard style guide is essential for producing great results in web design and style guides help in ensuring uniformity in website design styles. Website designers also create their own style guides to maintain consistency throughout the designing process.

Styles guides are essential when different website designers work on a single project and A/B testing is a great technique to discover alternatives in website designing. Every page on a website is vital for a web user and every web page should be perfectly designed. The overall design of a website should be approached from the perspective of target audience. Most of the website failures can be attributed to design preparation as well as implementation. A disorganized website will get low ranking in search engine results and having too little or too much graphics in a website will create lots of problems.

The amount of graphics in a web page will be determined by the profile of the target audience and the search engines rankings are affected by the length of the time the content in a website remains unchanged. A sitemap should be created for every website as it enables crawlers to easily access each of the pages of the website. Website designers should be equipped with elegant creativity in order to become rock star website designers. The advertisement links in a website should be blue and all information in a website should be clear, concise and informative. The website of an ecommerce store should be updated as often as possible and website designing is a good starting point in gaining trust.

Another website designing improving technique is to make sure that the typography of the content is suitable. The important parts of website should load very quickly and it is essential to continuously check website design for loading time. Website design should include relevant content for the visitor and for search engine optimization. The search engines love content that is relevant to keywords and the content should be broken up by small paragraphs. Navigation links in a website including text size, font size, and colour should be distinguishable from the rest.

Website designers should pay close attention to load time and layout of the website and improving website simply is not about design or search engine optimization. It is essential to design a website that is properly implemented and tested and website design should convince visitors to stay. The overall look of a website should impress visitors and a good website design relies on how the designer perceives it. Not every inch of our site needs to have colour or image and overloading the site with graphics or animation is not recommended. Page title is an essential element of website design and website designers should ensure that all pages are properly titled.

Font choice has a huge impact on how the site user is able to extract information from the website. Arial, Verdana and San Serif are three best font choices for website design and the font size should not be smaller than 10. The font size should not be larger than 14 points and effective website designing is a creative art. Website can be the best marketing tool for business and Flash ads are the difference between a mediocre website and really sharp looking website. Adding a shopping cart in a website is simple with PayPal and any special shopping cart software.

There is a lot of room for creativity in website designing and website designers should ensure that they have their own domain name. Every website should have favicon and websites without favicon lack professional look. The extremely subjective topic of website designing is an art form in its entirety and home page is the most important page in a website. An ideal website should have pleasing colours that are complimentary and it is essential to look things from web browser's perspective. The navigation links in a website should be clearly marked and there should be a web directory for easy access to links.

Professional looking and well designed website is a prerequisite for an online business venture. There are many new software applications that give us fully functional and good looking website for no cost. A talented website designer can offer stylish and unique design at cost effective price tags. SEO website design is necessary to ensure that business site performs well and the most significant element of website design is the proper usage of keywords. Relevant keywords should be used in the right places including title tag, graphic descriptions and slogans. Content in a website should be well structured so that search engine bots can access them quickly.

Domain name should be related to the target keyword phrase and it is an excellent method of optimization. Navigation menus used in the website should be search engine friendly and the usage of text based CSS3 is the best choice for improved search engine rankings. The images used in a website should be relevant to the content on the page and search engine friendly URLs should be included in a website. The speed of the web page influences search engine rankings and implementing good code structure is important. It is best to block unwanted pages with irrelevant content and these pages don't have any content value.

JavaScript and CSS should be externally placed so as to make the crawling process much faster. Social media engagement is another way to improve website design and search engine optimized page gives better results. A web development company converts website from simple website design to a multifaceted ecommerce site. Website designers pursue all possible avenues to make website interactive, user and search engine friendly. Most appealing and functional website increases Return on Investment and the most important factors that improve ROI are professional search engine optimization and website conversion rate optimization. Search Engine Optimization features the best internet marketing strategies and establishing better presence on the internet is dependent upon website designing.

Open Source Website Designing

Different types of open source technologies have evolved over the years including WordPress, Magento, Drupal, and Zen Cart. They have made developing high end web applications for small and medium sized businesses possible. The cost advantage, flexibility, developer community, and ease of usage are the principal advantages of open source website designing. We don't have to pay fees for using open source web technologies and using free software enables us to get the same quality of website designing for less money. Open source software allows us to integrate several other technologies and tools within the website.

It is easy to get free plug-ins or enhancements for the website and open source web technologies are effective in creating powerful and attractive websites. One option for getting a website up and running soon is to use open source website designing. Open source website designs are created as community collaboration and they have gained huge popularity very quickly. Open source website designing has some inbuilt features and they make use of the latest trends in website designing. Prebuilt system skeleton gives a head start to the developer within the website and more companies are becoming familiar with platforms such as Magento. Starting with an ecommerce platform minimizes the amount of time required to extend the finished website.

Content management systems are designed as a plug in model that allows functionality as well as design. Different content management systems feature shopping cart, blog, calendar of events, polls, contact page or search module. Content management systems have design frameworks called themes and they are available on the internet for free or minimal charges. Open source content management systems let us to construct websites by ourselves with the help of open source community. A proprietary content management system makes use of coding such as HTML, CSS, PHP and MySQL.

Web content management system is a complex application designed to provide complete solution for web publishing. Anyone without technical knowledge can operate open source content management system. Installation of web content management systems is very simple and open source website designers need a basic understanding of web hosting, domains and web. Anybody can use the content management system once it is installed and one administrator will be responsible for the website operation. Administrator manages the website, assign permissions to other users, and control what will be published on the site. The user interface of open source content management system is divided into two parts: front end and back end. Some open source content management systems are designed for specific tasks while some others are general purpose systems.

It is a well known fact that the web runs on open source software and GIMP is another classic open source website designing software. Some of the lesser known open source website designing software are KRITA, Visual Studio Code, UIKit, Pencil Project and KODEWEAVE. Krita is a fantastic graphics editor and more and more designers are using this website designing software. Krita brings life to digital paintings and it provides a traditional look to graphics and paintings. Visual Studio Code has scaled new heights of popularity and integration with Microsoft development tools is an elegant attraction of KRITA.

UIKIT is a lightweight and front end framework for developing fast and powerful web interfaces. Pencil has become a stable wire framing or prototyping web app and it has extensive collaboration feature. Pencil Project is still under development and the mission of Pencil project is to build an open source tool for creating diagrams. KODEWEAVE can be used as a standalone app for Windows, Mac, Linux, Chrome OS and Android. It is equipped with CSS pre-processors and KODEWEAVE can be integrated with an app called WebDGap. WebDGap application lets us to export code as a native desktop app and it is great for prototyping.

GrapesJS is known as a website builder and it lets us to edit designs online very easily as well as quickly. This site builder supports responsive design, code editing, preview modes, and undo/redo option. Another key attraction of GrapesJS software is a set of drag and drop predefined page elements. It can be included in a bigger web application, site builder service, and newsletter managing application. GrapesJS has proved its calibre as a capable page editor and open source website design software is great for website designers who are on a tight budget.

Some of the top rated open source website designing tools for website designers are Aptana Studio, Kompozer, Notepad++, Firebug, Quanta Plus and jEdit. Majority of the open source website designing tools have compatibility with expensive applications. Aptana website designing software combines powerful authoring tools for HTML, CSS, and JavaScript. Thousands of additional plug-ins are available in Aptana and Kompozer is a complete authoring tool. Best features of Kompozer are web file management and easy to use WYSIWYG (What You See Is What You Get) web page editing. Notepad++ is a source code editor and it is governed by GPL (General Public License). Firebug is a plug-in for Firefox web browser and it allows editing, debugging and monitoring Cascading Style Sheets.

Open source website designing technologies contain similar features to the costly web applications. They play a pivotal role in carrying out website projects very smoothly and Kompozer is perfect for people who lack technical skills. Kompozer helps us to create stunning websites without using code and the notable features of Kompozer are visible mark, CSS editor, FTP site manager and automated spell checker. GIMP is cross platform accessible for GNU, Linux, Windows, OSX, and different operating systems. The GIMP is a free application and graphic designers, photographers and illustrators make use of GIMP.

Different features of GIMP are flexibility, high level customization, colour management, and image manipulation. GIMP offers stylish as well as handy tools to a skilled website designer and it utilizes third party plug-ins. List of major features of Krita are intuitive user interface, brush stabilizer, brush engines, and PSD support. Krita is known as a finest painting application perfect for cartoonists, illustrators, website designers and concept artists. Inkscape is top rated professional quality vector graphics software and it works on Windows and Mac OS X. Inkscape can be used for developing creative graphics, illustration, logo, icon, diagram and maps. Best features of Inkscape include drawing tool, simple interface, multi lingual support and import of various file formats.

Fixed and Fluid Website Designing

Fixed design is the professional approach in which designer needs to define width of the page and popular websites like Yahoo and CNN make use of fixed design. Fixed website designing consists of text, images, and all other graphics elements defined in pixels. The first and foremost benefit of fluid website design is well controlled design of the website and designers will have total authority to make any changes without any problem. Fixed layout websites are easily viewable in mobile devices, PDAs (Personal Digital Assistants) and tablets. Fixed layout website is compatible with any kind of media device and it will run on any device.

A website designer using fixed website designing can get more control over the contents of the website. It empowers us to incorporate amazing background images within the website and fluid design enables viewers to choose how the web page is going to look on the basis of browser window as well as other display settings. Google and Wikipedia, whom we use extensively, are the best examples of fluid website designing. The top rung benefit of fluid layout is that it can utilize all available space and users can choose how the website will look. In the fixed layout website designing, each box inside is fixed by width rather than percent.

Fluid layout is also called as liquid layout and it can adapt to different screen resolutions. Many website designers prefer to use fixed layout because it is easier to achieve and it is more convenient to use. The webpage made by fluid layout is friendlier to visitors because it can adapt to user's settings. The space around webpage content is same in all the screen resolutions and it is often more visually appealing. Another advantage of fluid layout is that it can avoid horizontal scroll bar in small screen resolutions.

Fixed website designing requires horizontal scrolling and fluid website columns are relative to one another. Adaptive websites introduce media queries to target specific device sizes like tablets and mobile. A website designer should follow the differences among visitors including screen resolution, browser choice, extra toolbars and operating system. A 9600 pixel has become the most common standard in website designing because most website users are browsing in 1024/768 resolution or higher. According to website designing veterans, fixed layouts are easier to make and they are easier to customize in terms of design. If a website is designed to be compatible with the smallest screen resolution, the content will be wide enough at larger resolution.

Fixed layouts start with a specific size and it is determined by the website designer himself. They remain the same width regardless of the size of the browser and the fixed layout allows more control over how the page will look in different situations. Fixed width layouts allow the designer to make minute adjustments and they remain constant in different web browsers. The method chosen for website design will have an impact on design and fixed layout allows the designer to build pages that will look identical. Sites that require control over how the pages will look in every situation make use of fixed website design layout.

Fixed width layout ensures that branding of website is consistent and many website designers prefer a mixed approach. A fixed layout is one that uses a unit of measurement that doesn't depend on other factors. Websites in fixed layout appears with a constant size and the width of the various columns of web pages are specified using the measurement pixel. The web editor labels layouts "fixed", "layout", "elastic" and "hybrid" in Dreamweaver CS4. Both the elastic and liquid layouts in Dreamweaver are relative layouts and hybrid layouts are layouts that use a combination of different units of measurement.

The hybrid layout in Dreamweaver CS3 and CS4 use percentage of the total width of the page. It ensures that the web page fits within the confines of the browser window and hybrid layouts are better than relative layouts. Fixed website design makes it easy for designers to add new functionalities to the page and it gives designers more control over the design. Fixed designs are easier to develop and the best benefit of liquid design is that the layout will adjust to fit variety of situations. A liquid layout with its use of "em" or percents instead of pixels will be more accessible to viewers.

Another design approach is hybrid design where certain parts of the page are fixed and the choice of website design depends on lots of factors. The ultimate decision of website design is dependent on usability and the layout in responsive design changes based on the size and capabilities of the device. Responsive website design is a fresh concept in website designing and it is adopted for optimal viewing across variety of devices. It features layout in a readable form in an array of devices irrespective of pixel dimensions and screen resolutions. 960 pixel grid works well for fixed width designs and percentage based grids are known as fluid designs.

Responsive website design is an approach which suggests that design and development should respond to the user's behaviour based on screen size and platform. It consists of a mix of flexible grids, images, CSS media queries and the website automatically switches to accommodate for resolution when the user switches from laptop to iPad or Kindle. Responsively designed website should have the technology to automatically respond to the user preferences. Responsive website is a whole new idea of thinking about design and it is not just about adjustable screen resolutions. The entire website design is a mix of fluid grids, fluid images and smart mark up and creating fluid grids is a common website designing practice.

There are lots of techniques for creating fluid images including hiding portions of image and creating sliding composite images. One major issue that needs to be solved with responsive website designing is working with images. The most popular option of resizing images is to use CSS's max-width for an easy mix.

img {max-width: 100%;}

The idea of fluid images is to deliver images at the maximum size they will be used at and it is a good start to responsive images. If the original image size is meant for large devices, it slows download times and takes up space.

Trendy Personal Website Designing

Trendy personal website designing speaks a lot about the business owner and the design of personal website makes a huge difference. Website design trends change as time passes by and design patterns which were considered elegant before two years may get outdated in the upcoming years. An ideal website should have an appealing and trendy outlook and it should impress website visitors. Search engine optimization is the vital element for the success of personal website and website design plays a key role in search engine optimization. Professional website helps us to stand out as a professional and establish ourselves as an authority in business.

People notice the appearance of a website in the first glance and it should be eye catching to the visitor. Investing in personal website designing is the best way to guarantee successful online presence. Personal website should get the appreciation of online audience and neglecting the importance of personal website designing will minimize the chances of success. Personal website designing is the chance to show who we are and customized personal website design should be given utmost importance. Personal websites are dominating the internet world of today and most of the personal website pages are created as static pages.

Many of us prefer personal web pages to appear as dynamic pages and a professionally designed personal website will definitely attract visitors. A personal website should be search engine friendly and aesthetically created websites become a failure due to lack of smart search engine optimization strategies. Hiring a professional website designing company is vital as far as personal website designing is concerned. Companies should check the previous client list of the website designing companies and quality as well as professionalism characterise a typical personal website. The features of a personal website are attractive home page, easily accessible buttons, organized pages and quick download option.

The principle of "paying good and grabbing the best" is applicable to website designing companies too. Personal website is the best place to test a designer's skills and acquire experience in website designing. A personal website is for personal objectives, to show personal information, and profile. Personal website is for establishing personal brand and learning how to design personal websites need different skill sets. The first step in personal website designing is to get a domain and hosting and it is impressive to have self hosted site with an actual domain name. It is important to have a self hosted WordPress blog as a part of personal website designing and good domain name is an absolute requirement for personal website.

The best option is to make our domain name our first name+our last name.com and it is good for SEO purposes. If our name is already taken, we can use middle initial or middle full name in the domain name. The usage of numbers in domain is not recommended and dashes can be used only if they are really needed. .com (most preferred extension), .net, .org, .co, and .me are fine substitutes in domain name. Owners of personal website should select established and recognizable extensions that will help people to avoid confusion.

Domain's spelling should be easy to get and it will be easy to mention in casual conversation. Although buying domain and web hosting together is recommended, buying domain and web hosting separately is still an option. The small cost of website hosting gives personal brand and credibility to a personal website. Different options for web hosting include shared account, Virtual Private Server, or our own dedicated server. Shared hosting plan from Host Gator is highly recommended and it is very cheap and there will be no downtime. Many website designers have quick install options for installing things like WordPress and it takes only five minutes to install WordPress. The version of WordPress Host Gator comes with a short wizard that guides through the process of setting things up.

Some of us would like to ask the question, "should I go with one page or multipage design"? This is totally up to us and the number one objective of a personal website is to showcase the professional work. It is a good practice to link personal websites to professional's YouTube channel and podcasts. Going with multipage design gives us an option to showcase resume and a detailed look at our portfolio. A multipage design works best for getting hired, getting hired for scholarships and research opportunities.

About me page, biography page, resume page and contact page are the components of a successful personal website. It is a good idea to set "About me" page as the home page and I don't recommend listing email address, mobile number and address on personal website. A contact form, along with links to social media pages, is a better option in personal website. Graphic designers, software programmers, website designers and artists can utilize portfolio in a personal website. A professional looking for full time work or freelance jobs can make use of the "Hire me" page. Setting up blog in WordPress manually is really easy and having a blog is the perfect way to showcase our thoughts and creativity.

"About me" page will be the landing page of the personal website and it is the place where visitors will see first. We should highlight who we are, what we do, and what we are studying in detail with elegant portfolio. Showcasing the picture of the website owner is recommended and we can include quotes about our work from other people. Making email address clickable is really easy and making email address public should be avoided. One major attraction of WordPress is the large amount of themes available and the look of the website can be changed without knowing CSS or any other graphic design skills.

Some WordPress themes are made for specific types of sites including magazines and restaurants. Premium themes offer a lot more options than free themes and it gives more flexibility than free themes. Some of the recommended WordPress themes are Simple, Verbosa, Lovecraft, Ultra and more WordPress themes can be found at Themify. The theme Simple is splendidly versatile and it allows customizing each page to the maximum degree. Verbosa is another hot WordPress theme and it offers lots of room for creativity as well as imagination. Lovecraft is the pet theme of bloggers and typography, clean menu, and large image area help Lovecraft to stand out from other WordPress themes.

Site Architecture in Website Designing

Site architecture refers to the technical, visual as well as functional aspects of website designing. Website designers should never make compromises with site architecture and the site architecture ensures that website visitors find what they are looking for. It is a fact that visually appealing websites make a great impression and loading the website with graphic elements will eventually turn off visitors. Graphic elements don't contribute towards improving the visibility of the site or traffic conversion. Site architecture ensures excellent aesthetics and technology and a successful website design relies on functional aspects.

The technical aspects of website designing take care of the coding, script and layout of the design. The navigation of the website determines how functional it is and the visual aspect focuses on the colours, themes, images and fonts. Visual aspect complements content on the website and it just enhances appeal of the website in a spectacular way. The secret of successful website design lies on striking the right balance in site architecture. Website designers should ensure that visitors come to see more than just graphics and they browse conveniently. An ideal website design will take the site to higher Search Engine Results Page and the overall architecture of website includes usability, user interface design, web design and graphic design.

Developing the architecture of website is an essential part of the website design process and website designers should have a firm understanding of the goals of business. Knowing the business objectives of company will help website designers to make sound design decisions. Engaging with users is very important in website design and website designers should conduct research to understand their needs. Website design deals primarily with virtual space where as web architecture deals mainly with physical world. Architecture and website design possess lots of similarities and carefully edited design is applicable to both of them.

Concept sketches are used both in website design and architecture and website designers use wireframes instead of engineering schematics. Client designer interaction is a key factor in the case of website designing and a well informed client will be happier. Bold colour makes things appealing in a website design and architecture and website designers mix colours into the borders and typography. Too many details should be avoided in a website and website should be designed around the content. Website architecture is the planning of the technical, functional and visual components of a website. It is used as an effective tool by website designers and website developers in their endeavours.

The website architecture process is divided into project brief, website goal definition, defining target audience, competitor analysis and scenario mapping. Project brief refers to gathering data needed from the client and there is always scope for additional data gathering. Different steps involved in project brief are determining goals, brainstorming with the client, determining the target audience, determining competitors and meeting the decision makers. Clients should have a clear idea of who is their target audience and they should have a rough idea about the age, gender and location of the target audience. Website designers should discuss the deadlines, resource availability and organizational matters with client project managers.

It is crucial to understand the requirements of clients before starting a website designing project. The deliverable of the briefing stage is a written technical document and it should be verified by the client. The common goals of a website are monetizing the site, increasing the offline market share, and engaging customers online. Website designers will have a document consisting of a list of client goals and a list of project goals. Website designing specialists need to know their clients in order to ensure the success of the website designing project. There are several methods involved in competitor research including market participant polling, internet research and print media search.

The architecture of website affects the behaviour of visitors and search engine rankings in Google, Bing and Yahoo. If a visitor can't find the content within three clicks of the home page, he may immediately leave the website. It is recommended to create a three tier system for HTML website and the first tier will be the home page. The second tier in HTML website will be the sub categories and the third tier will be the sub categories of sub categories.

Site architecture of a website about website designing

First tier: Website designing

Second tier: Website designing, building, and marketing

Third tier: Search engine optimization, article marketing, pay per click

The content of a very large website will be more than three clicks away from the home page and it is better to create a sitemap containing all links to web pages. Website designers create sub categories to organize different sections in a website and all the CSS files can be placed in a sub directory called as CSS. Creation of sub directories enables finding, adding, or deleting files in website very easy. Content management systems make website easy to maintain without learning the HTML. Website designers should understand the benefits of having a content management system before building a website.

Defining the structure of website will determine the success of any online business by improving visitor conversion rates and search engine rankings. Website architecture is all about the hierarchy of the navigation and website designers should be able to view the content from the user's perspective. A website should be effective in leading the website visitors to the intended pages and it is advised to have a feedback before completing the website architecture. Ease of use is the principal key to effective navigation of a website and main navigation should remain visible whenever users wander on the site. Consistent design as well as placement are important in secondary navigation and different colours should be used for mouse over states.

Website designers need to ensure that drop down menus don't overlay important text and the navigation should be able to accommodate expansion. Number of clicks required to access any content pages should be set to minimum and usability testing helps us to identify where the content has not been properly organized. Too many links distributed throughout a main text will be annoying and a dynamic website controlled by CMS helps clients to manage the content in –house. An effective content management system lets website designers to update content, create pop ups, manage documents, swap images, and create new pages based on templates. Some search engines like the one and only internet giant Google indexes a portion of dynamically generated pages.

Free Website Designing Software

Some of the free website designing software doesn't need any coding skills to build a website. Highly customized websites created using free website designing software meets the needs of clients. The most common free website designing software is WYSIWYG (What You See Is What You Get) editors. No skills of coding is required to use WYSIWYG free website designing software and designing a website is so easy with the help of drag and drop features of free website designing software. Some free website designing software uses a text editor and it requires basic knowledge of programming languages like HTML and PHP.

The third type of free website designing software is the software that employs both WYSIWYG and text editor. The level of design knowledge should be considered before choosing a free website designing software. The extent of difficulty in using free website designing software varies from one software to another. Analyzing the different kinds of free website designing software is important in our endeavour of creating aesthetically pleasing websites. Some of the free website designing software which are sold like hot cakes in the market comes with preinstalled web templates. The objective of website should be clearly defined before using free website designing software.

As professional website designing is expensive, it is good to look for free website designing software. WebPlus is a popular brand of free website design software and it is very easy to use as far as novice website designers are concerned. Another excellent free website designing software is Nvu and it works on computers using Windows and Macintosh. One of the most talked about benefits of Nvu is that website designers don't need any HTML programming knowledge. It enables website designers to design an entire website by just using the free tools available with Nvu.

Predesigned templates and generic images are included in the stupendously popular Nvu free website designing software. With the entire free website designing software available, there is no reason for beginners to venture into the world of paid software. An amazingly stunning website can be created with the help of free website designing software within one day and it is the real power of free website designing software. Free website designing software helps us to choose the best colours, fonts, templates and background images available on the planet. Almost all free website designing software comes with an interactive tutorial and it explains how the software works. Free website designing software ensures that there is no need to invest hundreds of dollars on paid software.

Free website designing software enables online marketers to attain priceless means to establish business. The wide array of free website designing software ranges from highly technical HTML editor to WYSIWYG editor. The fundamentals of website creation can be easily completed by using a free website designing software. Small internet marketing companies can effectively utilize free website designing software. A successful free website designing software ensures that web site flows with aesthetics and professionalism.

The best thing about cheap website design software is that they can be tried free before purchasing. There are web hosting companies that provide free website designing software to their clients. Free website designing software can be used to create personal websites, ecommerce store, and internet products business website. A free website designing software helps website designers to design, establish and manage their website. An ideal free website designing software employs website designing applications that are easy to use. Some of the popular free website designing software are for starters and they are user friendly too. Top rated free website designing software are made for the beginners and its user manual describes basic website templates and addition of images as well as texts. The usage of website designing software is a fantastic aid in creating the online presence of business.

An effective free website designing software helps a company to stand out from their competitors. Using free website designing software will be time consuming if we are looking for fast results. The advent of free website designing software eliminates the notion that website designing is the domain of professional designers and coders. Selecting the best website designing application will be a little bit confusing as the market is flooded with thousands of applications. It is quicker, easier and efficient to create a site entirely using WYSIWYG (What You See Is What You Get) editor.

Desktop based free website builder is often found as the best tool for website building and some of the best free website designing tools are Wix, WordPress, Coffeecup Free HTML editor, and Joomla. Website designers rate Wix as the easiest way to build a website using WYSIWYG editor tool. Wix offers an opportunity to create websites online and it is considered as a quick method to design a website effortlessly. A simple option in Wix is to use the Wix ADI (Artificial Design Intelligence) website builder. Wix offers infinite opportunities for customization and there are literally tons of amazing templates available in Wix. According to website designers passionate about playing with colourful designs, Wix offers an impressive array of templates.

Wix is a cloud based website builder and it gives website designers great control over the appearance of the website. Features like newsletter and live chat can be included in Wix website builder and flexibility makes Wix website a popular website builder tool. There are two different versions of WordPress and the complex version can be downloaded from wordpress.org. Customization of templates and add-ons are the fascinating features of WordPress and the hosted version of WordPress is available at wordpress.com. It is easy to create blog, photo site, online store and templates using WordPress, the tinsel content management system.

The great benefit of WordPress is its ability to create an impressive and professional looking website. CoffeeCup Free HTML editor is a unique breed of website builder programs and it doesn't use content management system. Tag and code suggestions is a striking attraction of CoffeeCup Free HTML editor and the person using CoffeeCup Free HTML editor should have a basic knowledge of HTML. Joomla offers two versions just like its counterpart WordPress: build a site using the web app at Joomla.com or download the software from Joomla.org and host it ourselves. Huge collection of themes and extensions is the unique selling proposition of Joomla, the torch bearer of innovation in content management system.

Photoshop Basics

A person who wants to know more about digital photography and photo editing can learn Photoshop. Photoshop is the industry standard and it is known as a powerful image editing software with luminary reputation. Digital photo editing, logo creation, logo designing, eBook cover designing, CD cover designing, and conversion of photos into paintings are the major applications of Photoshop. The majestic attraction of Photoshop is that Photoshop is still being developed and improved every year. Some of the world's best digital photographers and digital artists make use of Photoshop.

Just being creative ensures success in the usage of Photoshop and Adobe has improved the usability of Photoshop. A step by step video course is necessary to learn the basics of Photoshop and learning Photoshop is not at all difficult. The basics of Photoshop include menus, tools, layer styles, layer adjustments, and filters. Photoshop video tutorials will help us to see how buttons, collages or even paintings are created. The easiest way to study Photoshop is by studying the interface and few of the elementary Adobe Photoshop tools. Vanishing point and image warp are the important tools in Photoshop and it enables us to easily clone images. Photoshop helps website designers to improve the overall appearance and feel of the website.

Learning to use Photoshop is one of the essential skills for a graphic designer and hobbyists who enjoy editing graphics use Photoshop as their preferred tool. Using Photoshop has a steep learning curve and Adobe Photoshop has a well designed interface. Beginner users of Photoshop are surprised at how quickly they can master fundamentals of Photoshop. Widely used painting tools in Photoshop are pencil, line, paintbrush, airbrush, eraser and gradient tools. The shape and hardness of round brushes in Photoshop can be tailored and the brushes palette menu allows resetting brushes.

Experienced website designers say that the most frequently used Photoshop tools are the paintbrush as well as airbrush. Beginner website designers will have to learn the basics of adjustment layers, saturation and hues.   A common application of Photoshop is the conversion of black and white photos into colour photos and vice versa. Photoshop training is a great investment for a professional website designer and it will help him to reach his full potential as a creative technocrat. Photoshop CS2 is the package for experts and novices who have learned the basics of the graphics editing software. Anything we want to do on the internet will be much easier if we have Photoshop training.

Photoshop is amazing graphics software that allows its users to create and manipulate images. It gives great advantages over designing with a paper and pen and a finished Photoshop product looks more professional than hand drawn product. The top rated features of Photoshop are versatility, user friendly interface, excellent training and variety of functions. Photoshop software was designed with consumers in mind and no specialized programming skills are necessary to use Photoshop. It makes use of WYSIWYG editor and the menu bar in Photoshop is similar to Microsoft Word.

As Photoshop is a popular image editing software, there are plethora of books, online tutorials, eBooks, and courses available on Photoshop. Photoshop can create endless variety of image editing and creation functions and the different kinds of photo manipulation activities are cropping the photo or changing the sharpness of the image. Another major benefit of Photoshop is that it allows manipulating both text and image on the same drawing canvass. Photoshop is very advanced when compared to other photo editing software and Photoshop Elements is a tuned down version of Photoshop. Photoshop Elements are designed for the casual photographers and they would have no desire to learn the complexities of Photoshop.

There are lots of plug-ins available in Photoshop and Photoshop Elements is available for the one by sixth cost of Photoshop. Photoshop Elements possesses simplified setting when compared to Photoshop and it has advanced colour management feature. Professional photographers can switch to the advanced version of Photoshop from Photoshop Elements. Photoshop has something for everyone and it will turn photo into something spectacular. Brightness and contrast tools available in Photoshop allow website designers to create colourful photos.

Photo restoration is one kind of project website designers can conceptualize in Photoshop software. The necessary tools for Photoshop are scanner, computer with Adobe Photoshop installed, colour printer and photo paper. Changing the background of the photo is another task that can be completed using Photoshop. Being a Photoshop freelancer ensures that they earn some extra cash and create some fantastic artworks. Different categories in Photoshop tutorial include photography tutorials, the basics category, special effects, texturing category, and website design tutorials. Photoshop software tutorials allow us to learn the tricks in video, graphics, films and special effects. This amazing graphics software lets us to open, crop, resize and view documents with great ease. Different tools available in Photoshop are helpful in enhancing, creating and retouching photographs.

Photoshop has links with Adobe software for media editing, computer graphics and authoring documentations. Photoshop Document (PSD) can be exported from Adobe Image Ready, Adobe Illustrator and DVDs. Different versions of Photoshop are Photoshop CS3, Photoshop CS3 Extended, Photoshop Elements 6.0 for Macintosh, Photoshop Elements 6.0 for Windows, Photoshop Express Beta, Photoshop CS6, Photoshop CC2014 and Photoshop CC 2017. Adobe Photoshop is a standard for professional graphic artists and it is one of the real prides of Abode. Photoshop is an ideal graphics tool for web designs, advertisements, desktop publishing and many other graphic works.

Painting directly on 3D graphics, wrapping of 2D images, conversion of gradient maps to 3D objects and better print quality are the coveted features of Photoshop. Common 3D format supporting, improved adjustment panel, fluid canvas rotation, file display options and 64 bit compatibility are other splendid features of the marvellous Photoshop. Photoshop software uses the colour models lab, RGB, binary bitmap, grayscale as well as duotone. It is capable of reading and writing images such as EPS, PNG, GIF, JPEG and other file formats. The traditional file formats of Photoshop are PSD (Photoshop Document), PSB and PDD (Photo Deluxe Document). Photoshop depicts a new revolution in the field of image creation and Adobe Creative Suite is used for various types of graphics and video editing.

Pricing for Website Designing

Domain name is an unavoidable cost included in website designing and some companies offer domain name for free. The next cost involved in website designing is that of hosting and animation and Flash increase the rate of website designing. Website designing costs can be divided into costs for design, search engine optimization, content development and ecommerce. Some website designers offer SEO services at cost effective price tags and an ideal website designer offers affordable services. Website designers either charge for each web page they create, for every hour or they charge an entire amount for the whole project.

Setting on an hourly rate is often an affordable option and it depends on the complexity of the design of the website. Complicated layouts and designs may cost more when compared with traditional website layout patterns. Many website designers who offer hourly rates are freelancers and they can create simple graphics on the website. Clients should ensure that they get the best return on investment from a freelance website designer. A per page rate is another common website designing price option and they are charged for every completed page. The main page will usually have the higher cost per page and creating the layout for main page needs more effort.

Per page rate is a great way to start website designing on a small budget and a complete package is the most popular website cost plan. A complete package will have all the necessary services to get the website running up on the web. Professional website designers create a well designed template for a price as low as $1000. A website design package for $1000 will include hosting as well as email and a package deal is the most desirable deal for the client organization. Hourly rate will be an option if the objective is to create a 2-4 page website and clients should ask website designer to provide timeline for completion.

Low cost with excellent services help a website designing company to stand out from the rest. Small website designing companies too make use of hourly rates and typical freelance website designers in USA charge around $100-$200 per hour. Per project pricing is rated as the convenient pricing option and it allows clients to choose from wide variety of options. Some companies offer website maintenance and website hosting free of charge in website designing packages. Working with overseas website designing companies will be a cost saving option since they charge only $15-$30 per hour.

One of the major benefits of working with a freelancer is that we are directly working with the person doing the actual work. The cost of website designing will depend on various factors such as business needs, design expectations, customer preferences, and functionality. The key aspect to determine the cost of website is the level of website design: number of pages created, multimedia and content. Website designing prices will increase if features like gallery, blog, and ecommerce site are included. A website designing firm with vast experience will significantly increase their rates and the most common mistake many companies commit in website designing pricing is that they don't think beyond website is built.

A trusted website designing company offers reliable maintenance, content management system and technical support. The important components of website designing package are search engine optimization, Google maps optimization and local search. Custom coding, premium designing, flexible content entry, website server space, 24/7 technical support, and domain name management are the key features of website designing package. The most expensive elements of website designing are slideshows, Flash animation, music players, CMS and user interaction. Expensive user interaction features in a website design package include commenting and ability to write customer reviews.

The complexity of the project determines the website designing cost up to a great extent and charging hourly for the projects is a transparent pricing strategy. The activities involved in a typical website designing package are planning, designing, coding, testing, and deployment. The per project pricing strategy is determined by how long it takes to complete the project and fair charging system is the specialty of per project pricing method. The per page pricing system is suitable for small business clients who want a brochure like web page. The per project pricing strategy is always fixed and it is necessary to differentiate cheap website design package from an expensive package since many companies prefer to choose cheap packages.

Small companies offer their website designing services for an amount less than five hundred dollars. A package beyond thousand dollars is often regarded as an expensive package and large website designing companies offer a higher price since they need to sustain all the expenses. The package offered by small website designing companies is often less since they work from their home office. They don't pay rent or other bills related to renting an office space and many of them utilize free website designing software.

If a client company is tight on cash, they can utilize free website designing packages like WordPress and Joomla. The typical website designing package consists of web hosting, creation of the site, ongoing maintenance, search engine optimization, web marketing and additional content. Web hosting is the least expensive part of the entire process and top rated hosting companies provide their service at low costs. The cost of a website will dramatically increase if video integration and Flash animation are included. Almost all website companies choose PayPal as their preferred payment partner in ecommerce site.

Online forms will be a great addition to a website and their prices are slightly higher when compared with other components of website designing. Some renowned SEO companies charge $100 per page for their services and investing in SEO is equally important just like investing in website designing. Using Google Keyword Search Tool costs nothing and it is recommended for companies on a low budget. Many companies spend $200-$300 per month for their internet marketing endeavours and the cost of website designing is outlined below.

Web hosting and domain name:$100

Creation of the basic site   :$500-$1000

Gallery page   :$500-$1000

Ecommerce   :$2500

Online forms   :$100

Search engine optimization   : $100-$300 per month

THANK YOU!

If you enjoyed this book or benefitted from it anyway, then I would like to ask you for a favour: would you be kind enough to leave a review for this book on Amazon.com? It would be greatly appreciated.